**Rex Jones II**, CSTE, TMap

# Getting Started With TestNG

## **A Java** Test Framework

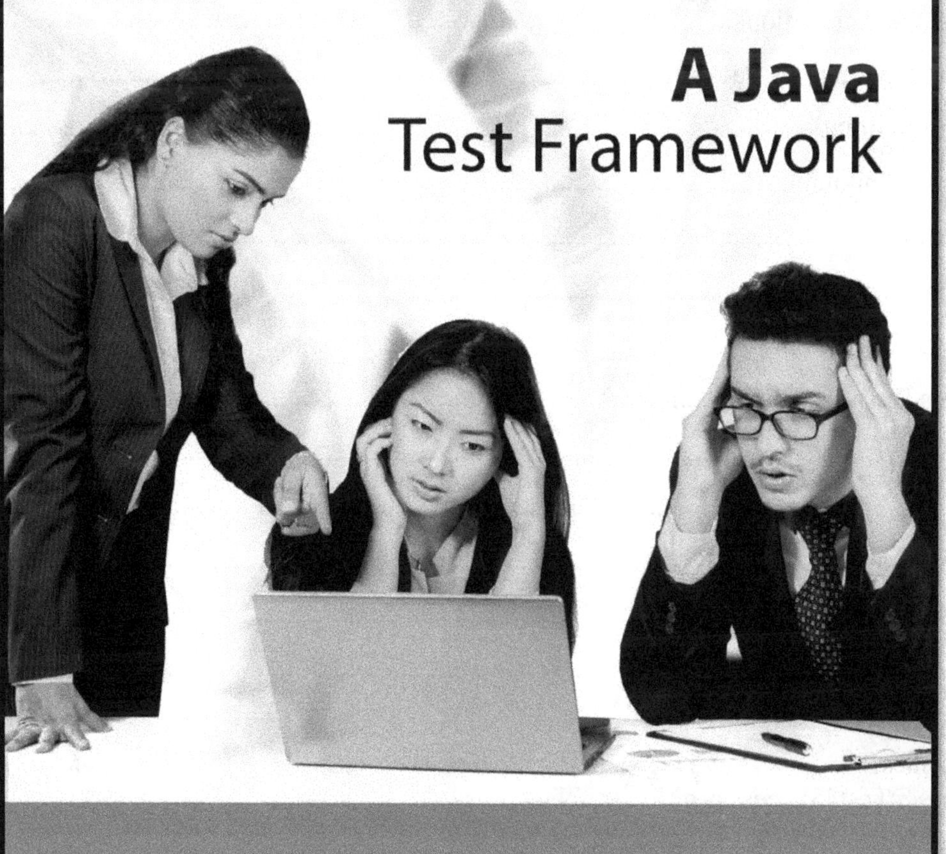

# Table of Contents



Skype: rex.jones34
Twitter: @RexJonesII
Email: Rex.Jones@Test4Success.org
LinkedIn: https://www.linkedin.com/in/rexjones34

# About the Author

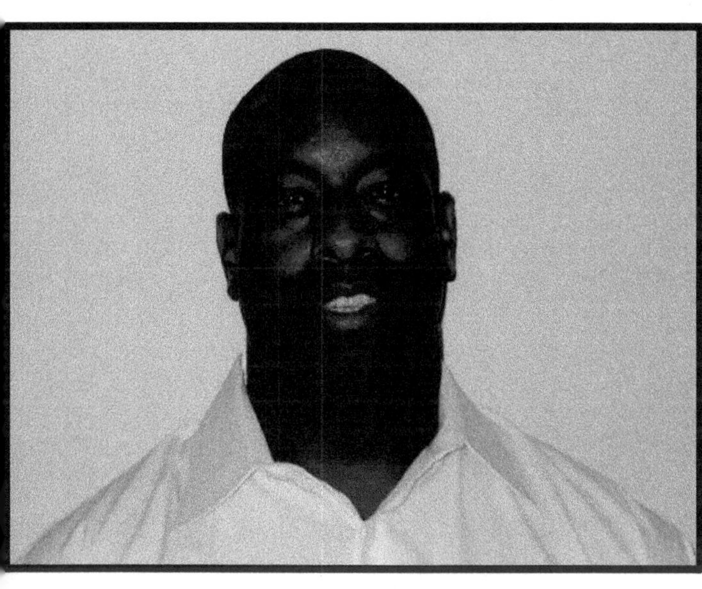

Rex Allen Jones II is a QA/Software Tester with a passion for sharing knowledge about testing software. He has been watching webinars, attending seminars, and testing applications over 10 years. Mr. Jones graduated from DeVry University with a Bachelor's of Science degree in Computer Information Systems (CIS).

Rex is an author, consultant, and former Board of Director for User Group: Dallas / Fort Worth Mercury User Group (DFWMUG) and member of User Group: Dallas / Fort Worth Quality Assurance Association (DFWQAA). In addition to his User Group memberships, he is a Certified Software Tester Engineer (CSTE) and has a Test Management Approach (TMap) certification.

Mr. Jones' advice for people interested in Automation Testing is to learn the programming language. This advice led him to write 4 programming books "(Part 1 & Part 2) You Must Learn VBScript for QTP/UFT" and "(Part 1 & Part 2) Java 4 Selenium WebDriver". VBScript is the programming language for Unified Functional Testing (UFT) formerly known as Quick Test Professional (QTP) and Java is one of the programming languages for Selenium WebDriver.

3 Tips To Master Selenium Within 30 Days
http://tinyurl.com/3-Tips-For-Selenium

Free Webinars, Videos, and Live Trainings
http://tinyurl.com/Free-QTP-UFT-Selenium

In addition to the 4 programming books, Mr. Jones wrote 2 more books. The 5[th] book is named Absolute Beginner (Part 1) Selenium WebDriver for Functional Automation Testing which provides a deep foundation of Selenium WebDriver. Finally, a 6[th] book named Getting Started With TestNG (A Java Test Framework). All books are available in Paperback, eBook, and PDF.

Skype: rex.jones34
Twitter: @RexJonesII
Email: Rex.Jones@Test4Success.org
LinkedIn: https://www.linkedin.com/in/rexjones34

# Rex Jones' Contact Information

Email Address: Rex.Jones@Test4Success.org
LinkedIn: https://www.linkedin.com/in/rexjones34
Books: http://tinyurl.com/Rex-Allen-Jones-Books
Twitter: @RexJonesII
Skype: rex.jones34

3 Tips To Master Selenium Within 30 Days
http://tinyurl.com/3-Tips-For-Selenium

Free Webinars, Videos, and Live Trainings
http://tinyurl.com/Free-QTP-UFT-Selenium

# Free Webinars, Videos, and Live Training

Mr. Jones plans to have **free** step-by-step demonstration webinars, videos, and live trainings walking people through concepts of Selenium and QTP/UFT from A - Z. The material will teach/train individuals the fundamentals of the programming language, fundamentals of Selenium and QTP/UFT, and important concepts of Selenium and QTP/UFT. All of the webinars, videos, and live training will be directed toward beginners as well as mid-level automation engineers.

**Sign Up to Receive**

1. 3 Tips To Master Selenium Within 30 Days
   http://tinyurl.com/3-Tips-For-Selenium

2. 3 Tips To Master QTP/UFT Within 30 Days
   http://tinyurl.com/3-Tips-For-QTP-UFT

3. Free Webinars, Videos, and Live Trainings
   http://tinyurl.com/Free-QTP-UFT-Selenium

Skype: rex.jones34
Twitter: @RexJonesII
Email: Rex.Jones@Test4Success.org
LinkedIn: https://www.linkedin.com/in/rexjones34

# Acknowledgements

I would like to express my gratitude to my wife Tiffany, children Olivia Rexe' and Rex III, family, friends, and the many people who provided encouragement. Writing this book took time and your support helped pushed this book forward.

Thank You,

Rex Allen Jones II

Rex Allen Jones II

3 Tips To Master Selenium Within 30 Days
http://tinyurl.com/3-Tips-For-Selenium

Free Webinars, Videos, and Live Trainings
http://tinyurl.com/Free-QTP-UFT-Selenium

# Copyright, Legal Notice, and Disclaimer



Skype: rex.jones34
Twitter: @RexJonesII
Email: Rex.Jones@Test4Success.org
LinkedIn: https://www.linkedin.com/in/rexjones34

# Chapter 1
# Unit Test Frameworks

Unit testing is a development process where developers test the smallest part of an application. Like most processes, unit testing can be time-consuming and tedious. Therefore, a unit testing framework facilitates the process. The Test Next Generation (TestNG) framework has an ability to execute an individual Test Script, execute a collection of Test Scripts (known as Test Suite), verify expected outcomes (Pass or Fail), and report results.

A Unit Test Framework should not get mistaken for an Automation Design Framework also known as Automation Test Framework. Unit Test Frameworks can be included within an Automation Design Framework. Some popular Automation Design Frameworks are Data Driven Framework, Keyword Driven Framework, and Hybrid Driven Framework. Automation Design Frameworks are utilized with different automation efforts such as Selenium WebDriver and automation tools like Unified Functional Testing (UFT) formerly QuickTest Professional (QTP). However, TestNG is a framework specifically designed for Java.

Another unit test framework designed for Java is JUnit. JUnit is part of a family of frameworks called xUnit. The xUnit family is a collection of unit test frameworks with a common architecture. Each framework has a structure for its respective programming language. For example, JUnit is structured for Java while NUnit is structured for .Net programming languages which includes C# pronounced as C Sharp. Both frameworks (JUnit and NUnit) are part of the xUnit family. The following is a list of a few xUnit test frameworks and their respective programming languages:

- AsUnit structured for ActionScript
- JUnit structured for Java
- NUnit structured for Microsoft.Net programming languages
- PHPUnit structured for Python

Nevertheless, not all test frameworks are part of xUnit. TestNG is not included in the xUnit family. Although not included in the xUnit family, TestNG was influenced by JUnit. As a result, TestNG adopted some of JUnit's concepts then added more features for testing an application. Some of the additional features are Data Driven Testing, Regression Testing, Dependency Testing, End-to-End (E2E) Testing, Integration Testing, and Cross Browser Testing. This book has a chapter on Dependency Testing, Data Driven Testing, and Cross Browser Testing. JUnit is the most popular test framework but TestNG is the most powerful test framework. The following are core functions of a Unit Test Framework like TestNG and JUnit:

- Create Test Scripts
- Generate Test Reports
- Generate Logs
- Read / Write Data in Excel

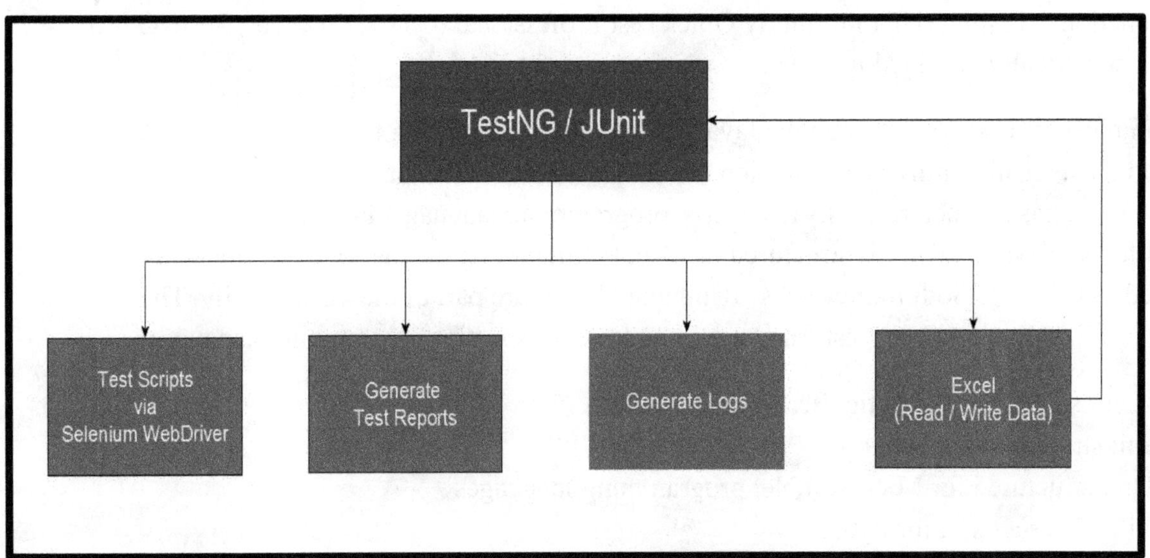


Figure 1.1 – Core Functions

Skype: rex.jones34
Twitter: @RexJonesII
Email: Rex.Jones@Test4Success.org
LinkedIn: https://www.linkedin.com/in/rexjones34

# Chapter 2
# Install TestNG

This book assumes Java and an Integrated Development Environment (IDE) such as Eclipse has been installed onto your system. If not, the internet has many resources with instructions along with my free PDF / eBook (Part 1) Selenium WebDriver For Functional Automation Testing. Eclipse IDE requires a TestNG installation to utilize TestNG features. The following are steps to install TestNG:

Steps To Install TestNG:

1. Open Eclipse
2. Load a Project "i.e., Hello World"
3. Click Help > Eclipse Marketplace

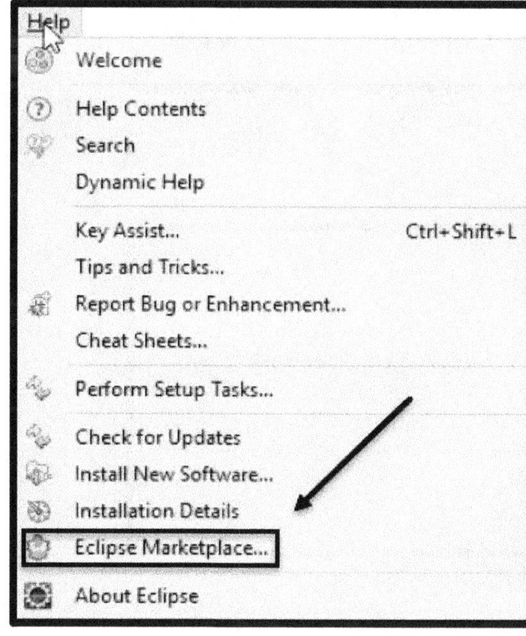

4. Search for TestNG, Click the Go button, then Click the Install button

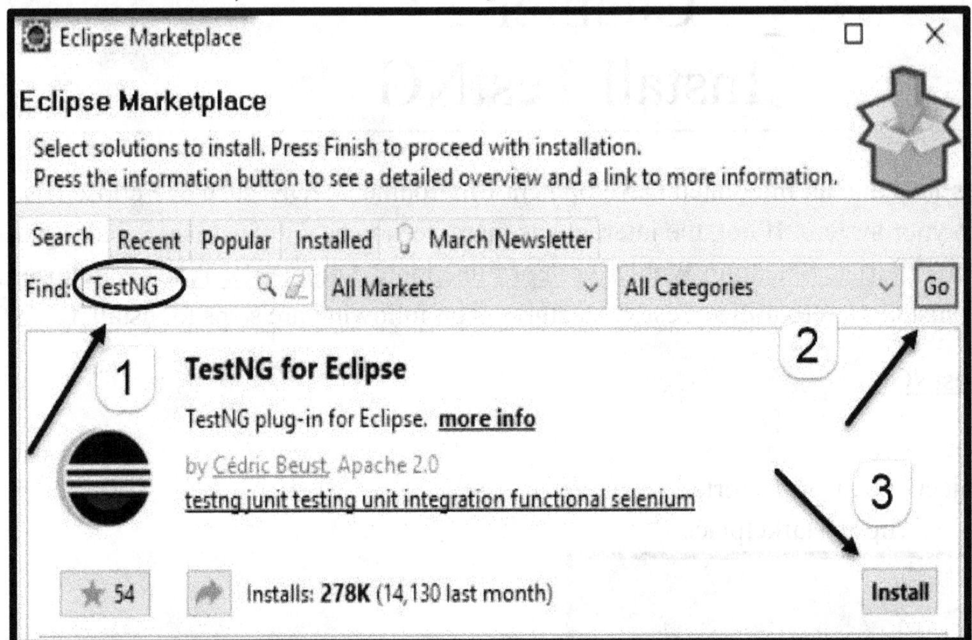


5. Click the Confirm button to confirm the following features:
    a. TestNG (required)
    b. TestNG M2E Integration (Optional)

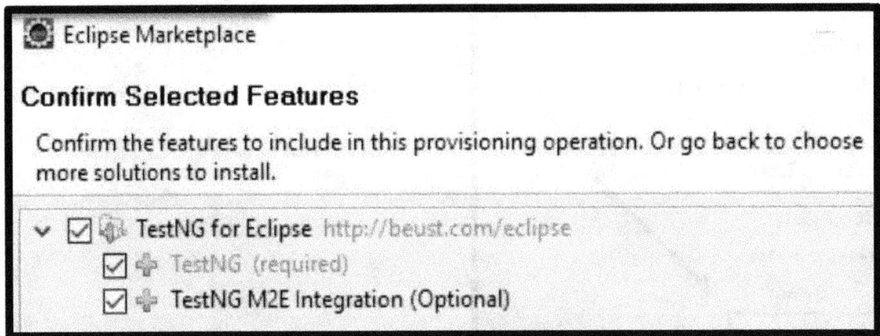


6. Click the radio button "I accept the terms of the license agreement"
7. Click the Finish button
8. Click OK if a Security Warning appears in a modal

9. Click Yes to restart Eclipse
10. Verify TestNG has been added
    a. Re-open Eclipse after restart
    b. Click Window
    c. Click Preferences

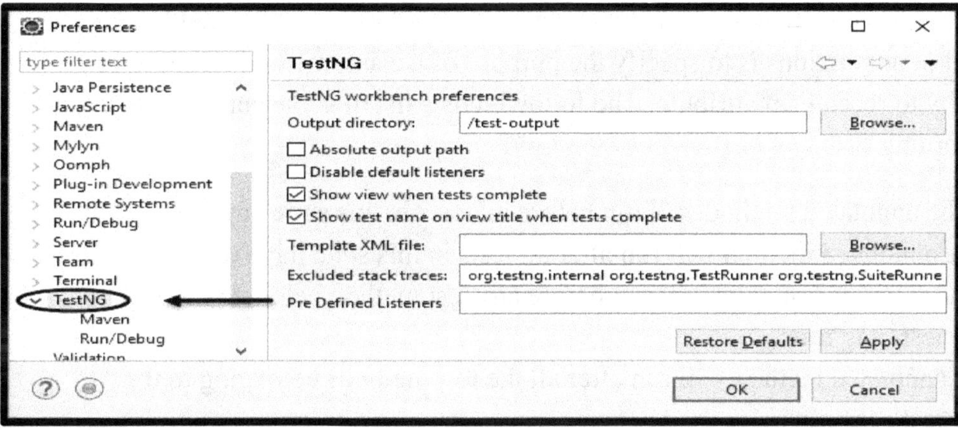

# Chapter 3
# What Are Annotations

The starting point of TestNG is annotations. An annotation provides metadata to the compiler. Metadata is data that describes data. All annotations start with an at "@" symbol followed by the annotation name. The goal of annotations is to specify the purpose of a class, method, or test. Annotations have the ability to receive an attribute. The following is a list of some annotation classes and their descriptions according to testng.org.

- @BeforeSuite – The annotated method will run before all tests in this suite have run.
- @AfterSuite – The annotated method will run after all tests in this suite have run.
- @BeforeTest – The annotated method will run before any test method belonging to the classes inside the <test> tag runs.
- @AfterTest – The annotated method will run after all the test methods belonging to the classes inside the <test> tag runs.
- @BeforeGroups – The list of groups that this configuration method will run before. This method is guaranteed to run before the first test method that belongs to any of these groups is called/invoked.
- @AfterGroups – The list of groups that this configuration method will run after. This method is guaranteed to run after the last test method that belongs to any of these groups is called/invoked.
- @BeforeClass – The annotated method will run before the first test method in the current class is called/invoked.
- @AfterClass – The annotated method will run after all the test methods in the current class runs.
- @BeforeMethod – The annotated method will run before each test method.
- @AfterMethod – The annotated method will run after each test method.
- @DataProvider – Marks a method as providing data for a test method. The annotated method must return an Object[][] where each Object[] can be assigned the parameter list of the test

method. The @Test method that wants to receive data from this DataProvider needs to use a dataProvider name equals to the name of this annotation.

- @Factory – Marks a method as a factory that returns objects that will be used by TestNG as Test classes. The method must return Object[].
- @Listeners - Defines listeners on a test class.
- @Parameters - Describes how to pass parameters to a @Test method.
- @Test - Marks a class or a method as part of the test.

# Chapter 4
# Import Annotations Package

Importing a package is a feature that allow a class to access members of another class. In the case of annotations, there are packages that contain annotation classes. The annotation classes must be imported so another class can use that imported annotation. There are some classes included in multiple packages. For example, Test is a class located in JUnit and TestNG while Parameters is another class located in multiple packages. The following is an example of several TestNG annotation imports:

```
import org.testng.annotations.Test;
import org.testng.annotations.BeforeMethod;
import org.testng.annotations.AfterMethod;
import org.testng.annotations.DataProvider;
import org.testng.annotations.BeforeClass;
import org.testng.annotations.AfterClass;
import org.testng.annotations.BeforeTest;
import org.testng.annotations.AfterTest;
import org.testng.annotations.BeforeSuite;
import org.testng.annotations.AfterSuite;
```

Figure 4.1 – TestNG Annotation Imports

Note: An automation engineer can use an asterisk (*) instead of the class name to import all classes. Here is an example of importing all annotation classes. **import** org.testng.annotations.*;

The following screenshot is a list of all classes via annotations package:

Skype: rex.jones34
Twitter: @RexJonesII
Email: Rex.Jones@Test4Success.org
LinkedIn: https://www.linkedin.com/in/rexjones34

Import Annotations Package

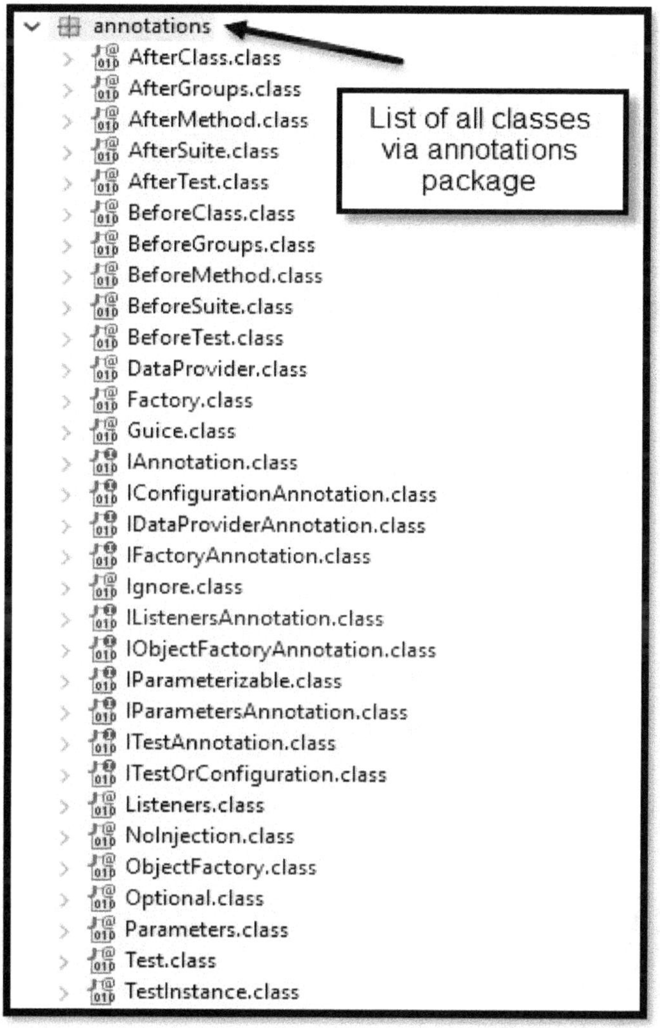

annotations
AfterClass.class
AfterGroups.class
AfterMethod.class
AfterSuite.class
AfterTest.class
BeforeClass.class
BeforeGroups.class
BeforeMethod.class
BeforeSuite.class
BeforeTest.class
DataProvider.class
Factory.class
Guice.class
IAnnotation.class
IConfigurationAnnotation.class
IDataProviderAnnotation.class
IFactoryAnnotation.class
Ignore.class
IListenersAnnotation.class
IObjectFactoryAnnotation.class
IParameterizable.class
IParametersAnnotation.class
ITestAnnotation.class
ITestOrConfiguration.class
Listeners.class
NoInjection.class
ObjectFactory.class
Optional.class
Parameters.class
Test.class
TestInstance.class

List of all classes via annotations package

Figure 4.2 – Annotations Package

# Chapter 5
# Create Annotations

The @Test Annotation is created to identify test methods. As a result, the annotation is placed one line prior to the test method. Annotations are case-sensitive with a syntax that must be followed but test methods can be any name. The annotations are created via New TestNG class modal or entered by the automation engineer.

## How To Add Annotations via New TestNG Class

In Eclipse, a New TestNG class modal is accessed multiple ways. The following are steps to access the TestNG class modal via project:

1. Right click the project name "e.g., Chapter_3"
2. Select TestNG
3. Select Create TestNG class
4. Select / Enter Source folder, Package name, and Class name
5. Check one or more the annotations
6. Click Finish

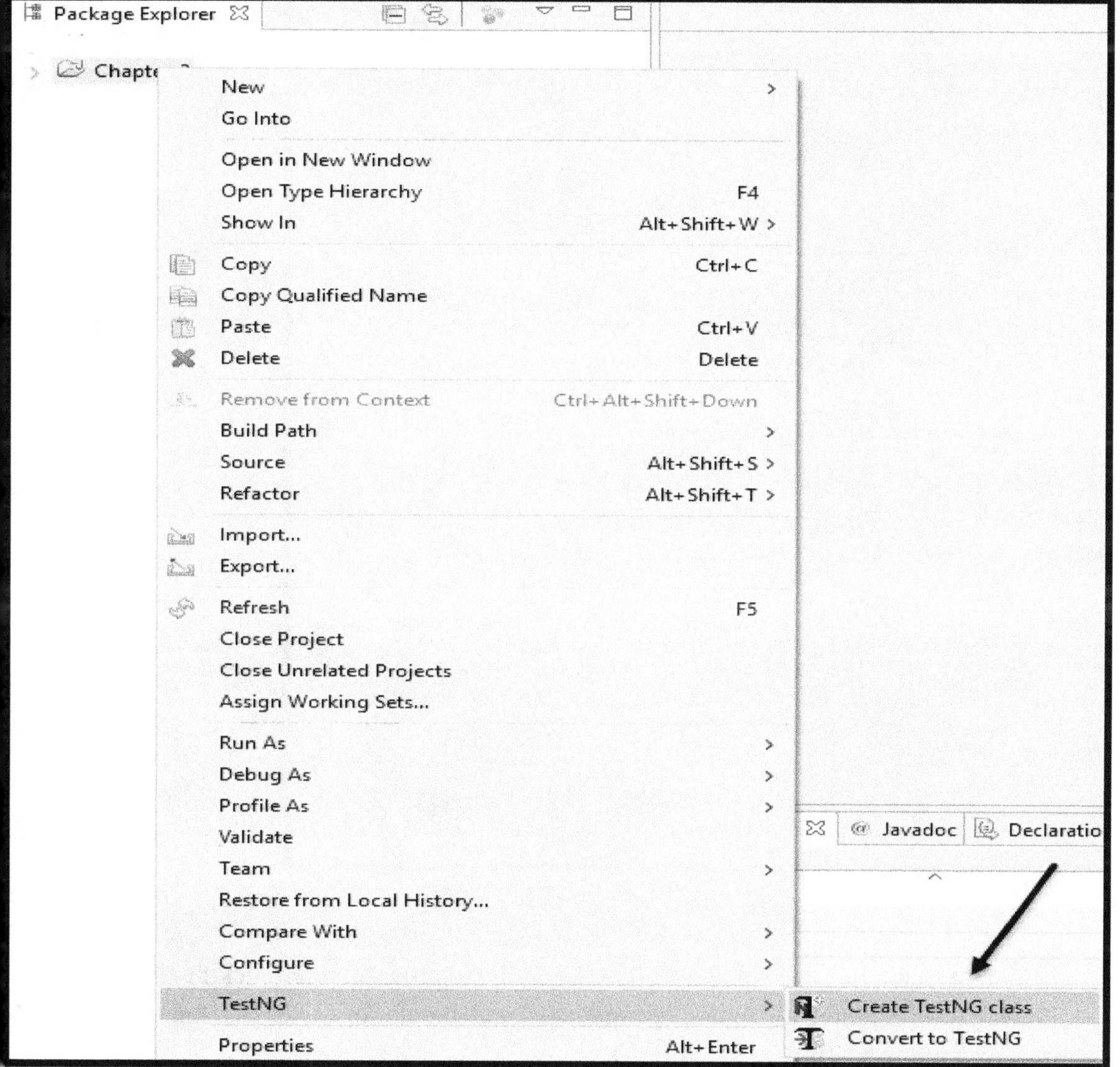

Figure 5.1 – Create TestNG Class

**New TestNG class**

Specify additional information about the test class.

Source folder: /Chapter_3/src [Browse...]
Package name: annotation [Browse...]
Class name: CreateAnnotation

Annotations
- [x] @BeforeMethod
- [x] @AfterMethod
- [x] @DataProvider
- [x] @BeforeClass
- [x] @AfterClass
- [x] @BeforeTest
- [x] @AfterTest
- [x] @BeforeSuite
- [x] @AfterSuite

XML suite file:

[Finish] [Cancel]

Figure 5.2 - TestNG Class Modal

<u>Note</u>: The annotations and imports are automatically created in the program after clicking the Finish button. The following is an example of a class, test methods, and annotations after checking the annotations checkbox from New TestNG Class modal:

Skype: rex.jones34
Twitter: @RexJonesII
Email: Rex.Jones@Test4Success.org
LinkedIn: https://www.linkedin.com/in/rexjones34

```
1  package annotation;
2
3+ import org.testng.annotations.Test;
13
14 public class CreateAnnotationsAutomatically
15 {
16   @Test(dataProvider = "dp")
17   public void f(Integer n, String s) {
18   }
19
20   @BeforeMethod
21   public void beforeMethod() {
22   }
23
24   @AfterMethod
25   public void afterMethod() {
26   }
27
28   @DataProvider
29   public Object[][] dp() {
30     return new Object[][] {
31       new Object[] { 1, "a" },
32       new Object[] { 2, "b" },
33     };
34   }
35   @BeforeClass
36   public void beforeClass() {
37   }
38
39   @AfterClass
40   public void afterClass() {
41   }
42
43   @BeforeTest
44   public void beforeTest() {
45   }
46
47   @AfterTest
48   public void afterTest() {
49   }
50
51   @BeforeSuite
52   public void beforeSuite() {
53   }
54
55   @AfterSuite
56   public void afterSuite() {
57   }
58
59 }
```

All of the imports except for one has been minimized. Notice line number shows 3 then 13

Figure 5.3 – TestNG Annotations

Note: Lines 3 – 12 have imports. However, lines 4 – 12 are minimized so all of the imports are not visible. The remaining lines are shown by clicking the plus icon (+) next to line 3.

## How Automation Engineers Write Annotations

In the previous example, all of the annotations were checked in the New TestNG Class modal. Generally, all annotations are not checked or written by an automation engineer. Only the annotations necessary for testing is utilized. An automation engineer can write any of the annotations from the list of annotations. The following is a Test annotation "@Test" example:

```
1  package annotation;
2
3  public class WriteAnnotations
4  {
5      @Test
6      public void testFirstScript ()
7      {
8          System.out.println("This is the first test script");
9      }
10 }
```

Figure 5.4 – Test Annotation

Notice, the error at line 5 for the Test annotation "@Test". A TestNG library and test annotation import must be added to resolve the error. Eclipse displays several solutions by hovering over the error. The following shows how to add an import.

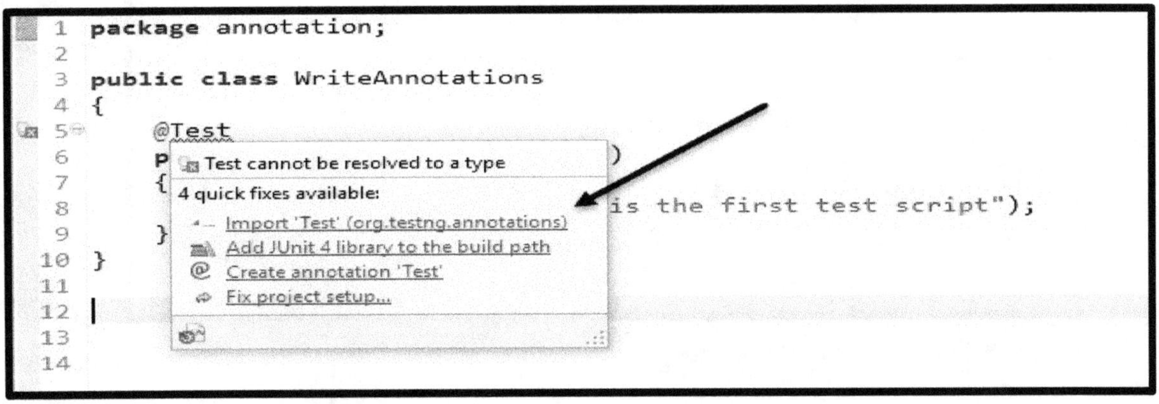

```
1  package annotation;
2
3  public class WriteAnnotations
4  {
5      @Test
6      p   Test cannot be resolved to a type          )
7      {   4 quick fixes available:
8              Import 'Test' (org.testng.annotations)    is the first test script");
9      }       Add JUnit 4 library to the build path
10 }           Create annotation 'Test'
11             Fix project setup...
12
13
14
```

Figure 5.5 – Select Test Annotation Import

Skype: rex.jones34
Twitter: @RexJonesII
Email: Rex.Jones@Test4Success.org
LinkedIn: https://www.linkedin.com/in/rexjones34

```
1  package annotation;
2
3  import org.testng.annotations.Test;
4
5  public class WriteAnnotations
6  {
7      @Test
8      public void testFirstScript ()
9      {
10         System.out.println("This is the first test script");
11     }
12 }
```

Figure 5.6 – Test Annotation Import

- The option “Import ‘Test’ (org.testng.annotations)” was selected to import the Test annotation
- Line 3 automatically populates the program with an import to resolve the error

Note: In this example, TestNG was added as a library to the Project Explorer before importing the Test annotation. The following is a screenshot of the TestNG library:

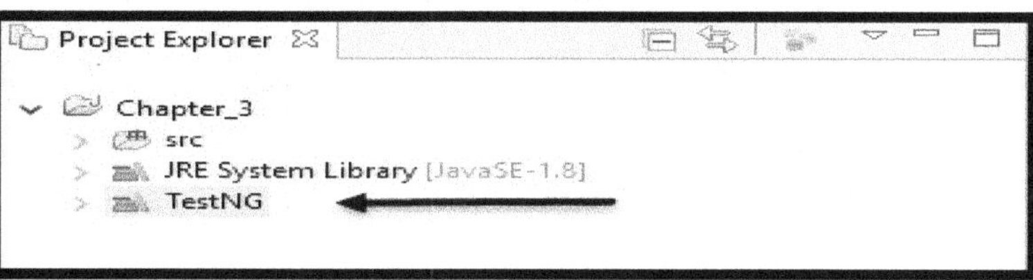


Figure 5.7 – TestNG Library

# Chapter 6
# Execute Annotations

The annotations can be located anywhere in the class and still execute according to a predefined order. TestNG contains an in-built mechanism for executing annotations. According to Next Generation Java ™ Testing TestNG and Advanced Concepts, every time a method is annotated with one of these annotations, it will run at the following time (page 20):

- @BeforeSuite / @AfterSuite – before a suite starts / after all the test methods in a certain suite have been run
- @BeforeTest / @AfterTest – before a test starts / after all the test methods in a certain test have been run
- @BeforeClass / @AfterClass – before a test class starts / after all the test methods in a certain class have been run
- @BeforeMethod / @AfterMethod – before a test method is run / after a test method has been run

The following is an example illustrating an annotation execution order:

```
@Test // This is a test method
public void testMethod ()
{
    System.out.println("@Test - This is a test method");
}

@BeforeMethod // Executes before each test
public void beforeMethod()
{
    System.out.println("@BeforeMethod - Executes before each test method");
}

@AfterMethod
public void afterMethod()
{
    System.out.println("@AfterMethod - Executes after each test method");
}

@BeforeClass
public void beforeClass()
{
    System.out.println("@BeforeClass - Executes first in the class");
}

@AfterClass
public void afterClass()
{
    System.out.println("@AfterClass - Executes last in the class");
}

@BeforeTest
public void beforeTest()
{
    System.out.println("@BeforeTest - Executes before all test methods");
}

@AfterTest
public void afterTest()
{
    System.out.println("@AfterTest - Executes after all test methods");
}

@BeforeSuite
public void beforeSuite()
{
    System.out.println("@BeforeSuite - Executes first in the suite");
}

@AfterSuite
public void afterSuite()
{
    System.out.println("@AfterSuite - Executes last in the suite");
}
```

Figure 6.1 – Annotation Execution Order

**Program Output**:

```
@BeforeSuite - Executes first in the suite
```

```
@BeforeTest - Executes before all test methods
@BeforeClass - Executes first in the class
@BeforeMethod - Executes before each test method
@Test - This is a test method
@AfterMethod - Executes after each test method
@AfterClass - Executes last in the class
@AfterTest - Executes after all test methods
@AfterSuite - Executes last in the suite
```

- Lines 7, 13, 19, 25, 31, 37, 43, 49, and 55 contain TestNG annotations
- The program displays the annotations in the following order: @Test, @BeforeMethod, @AfterMethod, @BeforeClass, @AfterClass, @BeforeTest, @AfterTest, @BeforeSuite, @AfterSuite
- The annotations execute in the following predefined order: @BeforeSuite, @BeforeTest, @BeforeClass, @BeforeMethod, @Test, @AfterMethod, @AfterClass, @AfterTest, @AfterSuite

The test annotations "@Test" execute in a predefined order if multiple Test annotations are created in a program. The following is an example execution of multiple Test annotations in a single class.

```
1 package annotation;
2
3 import org.testng.annotations.*;
4
5 public class ExecuteTestAnnotations
6 {
7     @Test
8     public void testInternetExplorer ()
9     {
10        System.out.println("Test Script 3 - Cross Browser Testing in Internet Explorer");
11    }
12
13    @Test
14    public void testFirefox ()
15    {
16        System.out.println("Test Script 1 - Cross Browser Testing in Firefox");
17    }
18
19    @Test
20    public void testGoogle ()
21    {
22        System.out.println("Test Script 2 - Cross Browser Testing in Google");
23    }
24 }
```

Figure 6.2 – Execution Order For Multiple Test Annotations

**Program Output**:

```
Test Script 1 - Cross Browser Testing in Firefox
Test Script 2 - Cross Browser Testing in Google
Test Script 3 - Cross Browser Testing in Internet Explorer
```

- Lines 7, 13, and 19 display multiple Test annotations "@Test" which identify test methods at lines 8, 14, and 20
- The program displays the test methods in the following order: testInternetExplorer, testFirefox, and testGoogle
- The test methods execute in the following order: testFirefox, testGoogle, then testInternetExplorer

Note: The test methods were executed in alphabetical order according to the method's name. As a result, it is beneficial to pass a priority attribute to each test annotation. The following is an example using a priority attribute to specify an execution order:

```
1 package annotation;
2
3 import org.testng.annotations.*;
4
5 public class OrderTestAnnotations
6 {
7     @Test (priority = 2)
8     public void testInternetExplorer ()
9     {
10        System.out.println("Test Script 3 - Cross Browser Testing in Internet Explorer");
11    }
12
13    @Test (priority = 3)
14    public void testFirefox ()
15    {
16        System.out.println("Test Script 1 - Cross Browser Testing in Firefox");
17    }
18
19    @Test (priority = 1)
20    public void testGoogle ()
21    {
22        System.out.println("Test Script 2 - Cross Browser Testing in Google");
23    }
24 }
```

Figure 6.3 – Priority Attribute

Program Output:

```
Test Script 2 - Cross Browser Testing in Google
Test Script 3 - Cross Browser Testing in Internet Explorer
Test Script 1 - Cross Browser Testing in Firefox
```

- Lines 7, 13, and 19 include a priority attribute within the Test annotations. The priority attribute sets the precedence for each test method on lines 8, 14, and 20

Skype: rex.jones34
Twitter: @RexJonesII
Email: Rex.Jones@Test4Success.org
LinkedIn: https://www.linkedin.com/in/rexjones34

- Execution order for the test methods are testGoogle (line 20), testInternetExplorer (line 8), then testFirefox (line 14). As a result, the Program Output displays Test Script 2, Test Script 3, and Test Script 1

The following is an example displaying the execution order for multiple TestNG annotations:

```
package annotation;

import org.testng.annotations.*;

public class ExecuteMostAnnotations
{
    @BeforeMethod // Execute before each test (i.e., @Test)
    public void openBrowser()
    {
        System.out.println("Open Browser");
    }

    @AfterMethod // Execute after each test (i.e., @Test)
    public void closeBrowser()
    {
        System.out.println("Close Browser \n");
    }

    @BeforeTest // Before all test scripts are executed
    public void connectDataBase()
    {
      System.out.println("Connect to a Database \n");
    }

    @AfterTest // After all test scripts are executed
    public void disconnectDataBase()
    {
        System.out.println("Disconnect from the Database");
    }

    @Test (priority = 1)
    public void testFirefox ()
    {
        System.out.println("Test Script 1 - Cross Browser Testing in Firefox");
    }

    @Test (priority = 2)
    public void testGoogle ()
    {
        System.out.println("Test Script 2 - Cross Browser Testing in Google");
    }

    @Test (priority = 3)
    public void testInternetExplorer ()
    {
        System.out.println("Test Script 3 - Cross Browser Testing in Internet Explorer");
    }
}
```

Figure 6.4 – TestNG Annotations And Priority Attribute

**Program Output**:

```
Connect to a Database

Open Browser
Test Script 1 - Cross Browser Testing in Firefox
Close Browser

Open Browser
Test Script 2 - Cross Browser Testing in Google
Close Browser

Open Browser
Test Script 3 - Cross Browser Testing in Internet Explorer
Close Browser

Disconnect from the Database
```

- Lines 7, 13, 19, 25, 31, 37, and 43 contain different TestNG annotations. Lines 31, 37, and 43 are the test annotations
- The annotations execute in the following order:
  - **Line 19**
    @BeforeTest
  - **Line 7, Line 31, Line 13**
    @BeforeMethod, @Test – testFirefox, @AfterMethod
  - **Line 7, Line 37, Line 13**
    @BeforeMethod, @Test – testGoogle, @AfterMethod
  - **Line 7, Line 43, Line 13**
    @BeforeMethod, @Test – testInternetExplorer, @AfterMethod
  - **Line 25**
    @AfterTest

# Chapter 7
# Assertions

Assertions are methods used to verify whether a test Pass or Fail. The support is carried out through an Assert class which contain over 50 methods. Hard Assertions and Soft Assertions are 2 types of assertions. A Hard Assertion stops executing a Test Script when it Fails then places the test in a report. Contrarily, Soft Assertions do not stop executing a Test Script when it Fails. The Test Script continues to run then places the failed test in a report. Some of the Assertion methods are below:

| **Assertion** | **Description** |
|---|---|
| assertEquals | Asserts that 2 Data Types are equal |
| assertEqualsNoOrder | Asserts that 2 Arrays have the same elements |
| assertFalse | Asserts a condition is false |
| assertNotNull | Asserts an object is not null |
| assertNotSame | Asserts 2 objects don't refer to the same object |
| assertNull | Asserts an object is null |
| assertSame | Asserts 2 objects refer to the same object |
| assertThrows | Asserts a runnable throws an exception |
| assertTrue | Asserts a condition is true |
| Fail | Fails a test |

Figure 7.1 – Assertion Methods and Descriptions

Skype: rex.jones34
Twitter: @RexJonesII
Email: Rex.Jones@Test4Success.org
LinkedIn: https://www.linkedin.com/in/rexjones34

The syntax for most Assertion methods are String actualValue, String expectedValue, String message. Messages are optional and only displayed if the Assertion fail. The following screenshots show Syntax, Description, and automation code for Assert.assertEquals() method.

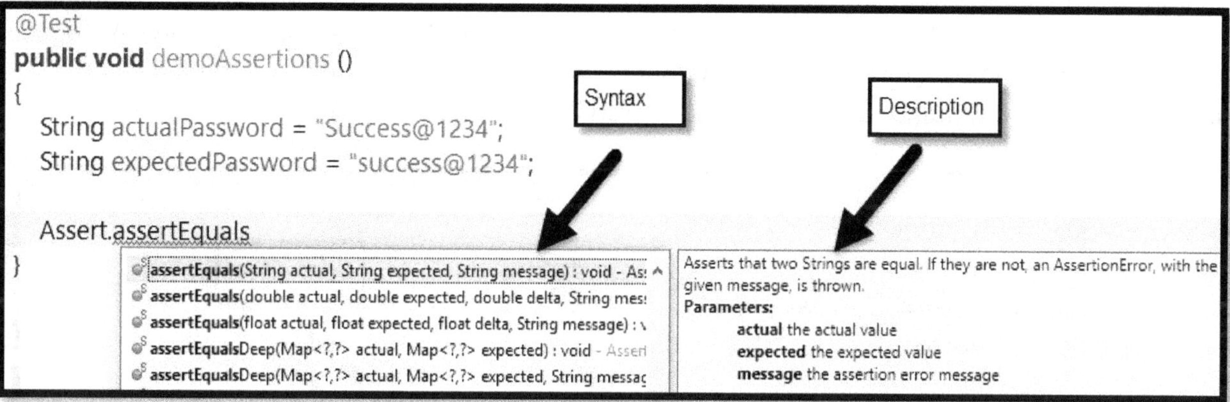


Figure 7.2 – Assert.assertEquals Syntax and Description

```
@Test
public void demoAssertions ()
{
    String actualPassword = "Success@1234";
    String expectedPassword = "success@1234";

    Assert.assertEquals(actualPassword, expectedPassword,
                        "The Actual And Expected Values DO NOT Match");
}
```

Figure 7.3 – Example Code Using Assert.assertEquals

Figure 7.3 shows an example of Assert.assertEquals() where 2 strings are asserted to be equal on Line 144. The 2 strings are actualPassword and expectedPassword with a message that states "The Actual And Expected Values DO NOT Match" on Line 145. In this example, the verification Fails because both String values are not equal. The message "The Actual And Expected Values DO NOT Match" will show up on a report. Notice on Line 141 'Success' begins with an uppercase 'S' while 'success' has a lowercase 's' on Line 142. The following screenshots is another Assertion method that asserts whether a condition is true via Assert.assertTrue().

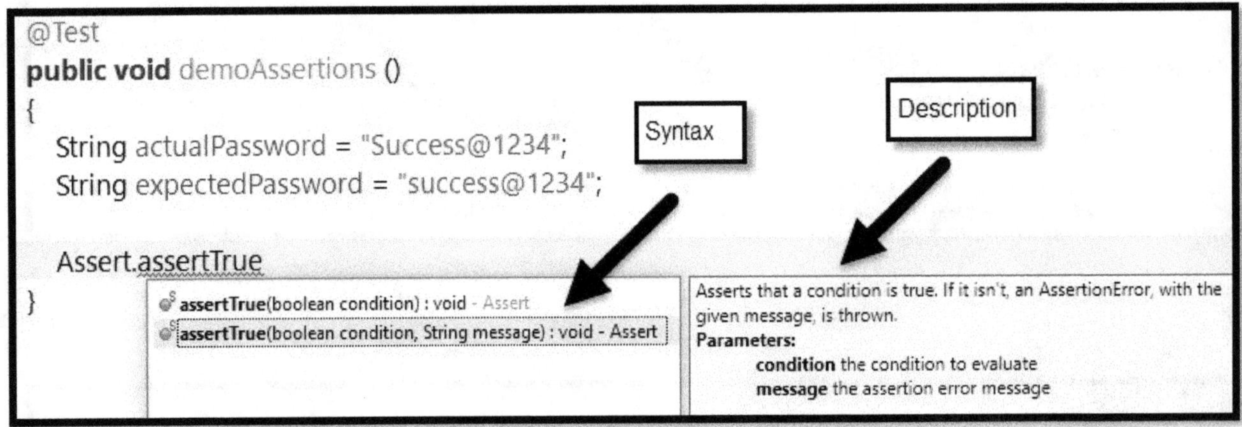


Figure 7.4 – Assert.assertTrue Syntax and Description

Skype: rex.jones34
Twitter: @RexJonesII
Email: Rex.Jones@Test4Success.org
LinkedIn: https://www.linkedin.com/in/rexjones34

```
138 @Test
139 public void demoAssertions ()
140 {
141    String actualPassword = "Success@1234";
142    String expectedPassword = "success@1234";
143
144    Assert.assertTrue(actualPassword.equalsIgnoreCase(expectedPassword),
145                      "The Actual And Expected Values DO NOT Match");
146 }
```

Figure 7.5 – Example Code For Assert.assertTrue

Figure 7.4 shows the Syntax and Description for Assert.assertTrue. Notice there are 2 assertTrue() methods in the screenshot. Both methods are similar but the second method has a parameter of String message. The second method is used in example Figure 7.5 with a message. Recall messages are only displayed if the Assertion fail like Figure 7.3. In this example, the message is not displayed because the test Pass. The equalsIgnoreCase() method enables this test to Pass although Line 141 and 142 contain different String values. The case consideration for Success and success is ignored due to the equalsIgnoreCase() method.

Note: The test would have failed if an equals() method was used rather than equalsIgnoreCase(). As you can see, an automation engineer has the option of deciding which Assertion method and Java method to use for verifying whether a test Pass or Fail.

# Chapter 8
# Dependency Testing

Per Tutorials Point, Dependency Testing is a testing technique in which an application's requirements are pre-examined for an existing software. The impacted areas of the application are also tested when testing the new features or existing features. TestNG offers the following dependency attributes via @Test Annotation when a test depends on another test:

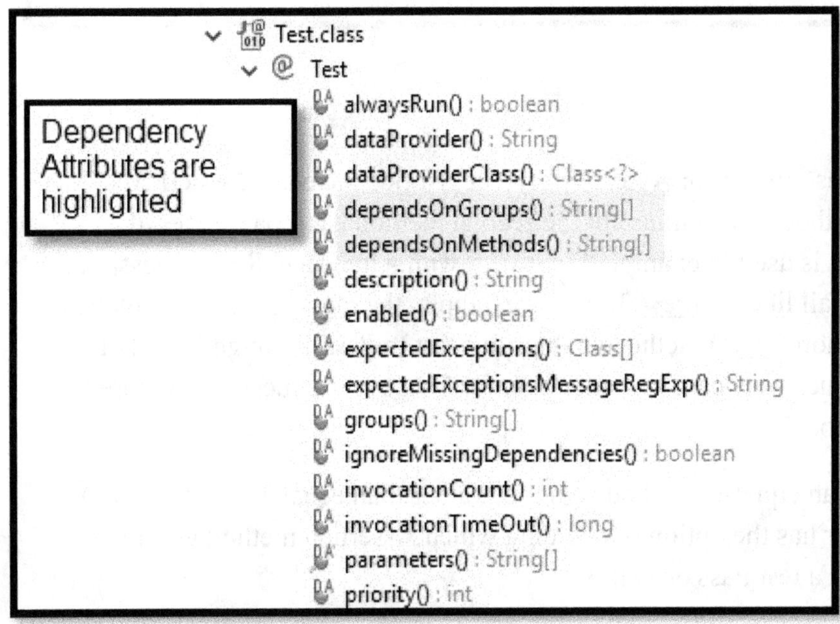


Figure 8.1 – Dependency Attributes via @Test

Skype: rex.jones34
Twitter: @RexJonesII
Email: Rex.Jones@Test4Success.org
LinkedIn: https://www.linkedin.com/in/rexjones34

- dependsOnMethods() – contains a method or list of methods that a different method depends on
- dependsOnGroups() – contains a group or list of groups that a different group depends on

Similarly, to the priority attribute, dependsOnMethods and dependsOnGroups enable execution to run in a specific order. In addition to the execution order, TestNG will skip a test that depends on a Failed or Skipped test. For example, the following 2 screenshots show how 2 tests Pass after a Skipped test (Figures 8.2 and 8.3). Subsequently, the next 2 screenshots show how the same 2 tests are Skipped via dependsOnMethods (Figures 8.4 and 8.5).

Note: The focal point of this chapter is dependsOnMethods(). Other Test Types such as Smoke Testing, Regression Testing, End-to-End (E2E) Testing, etc. can be carried out using groups() and dependsOnGroups().

```
@Test (priority = 1)
public void signIn ()
{
   throw new SkipException("Skip Until We Get More UserNames");
}

@Test (priority = 2)
public void registerUser ()
{
   System.out.println("Register A User");
}

@Test (priority = 3)
public void signOut ()
{
   System.out.println("Sign Out");
}
```

Figure 8.2 – Example Code With A Skipped Method And No Dependency Attribute

```
Register A User
Sign Out


PASSED: registerUser
PASSED: signOut
SKIPPED: signIn
org.testng.SkipException: Skip Until We Get More UserNames

signIn (0.007 s)
registerUser (0.001 s)
signOut (0 s)
```

Figure 8.3 – Results From Executing A Skipped Method Without A Dependency Attribute

Figure 8.2 shows the signIn() method is skipped using a SkipException via Line 37. As a result, in Figure 8.3, the signIn() method is SKIPPED while registerUser() and signOut() PASSED. Both methods PASSED because they are independent of the signIn() method which has a priority = 1.

- Eclipse's Console displays a print statement for Register A User and Sign Out. Also a message states "Skip Until We Get More UserName" in the Console
- TestNG Results tab shows a yellow icon for skipped signIn method and green icon for registerUser and signOut methods

Skype: rex.jones34
Twitter: @RexJonesII
Email: Rex.Jones@Test4Success.org
LinkedIn: https://www.linkedin.com/in/rexjones34

```
@Test ()
public void signIn ()
{
   throw new SkipException("Skip Until We Get More UserNames");
}

@Test (dependsOnMethods = {"signIn"})
public void registerUser ()
{
   System.out.println("Register A User");
}

@Test (dependsOnMethods = {"signIn"})
public void signOut ()
{
   System.out.println("Sign Out");
}
```

Figure 8.4 – Example Code With A Skipped Method And dependsOnMethods Attribute

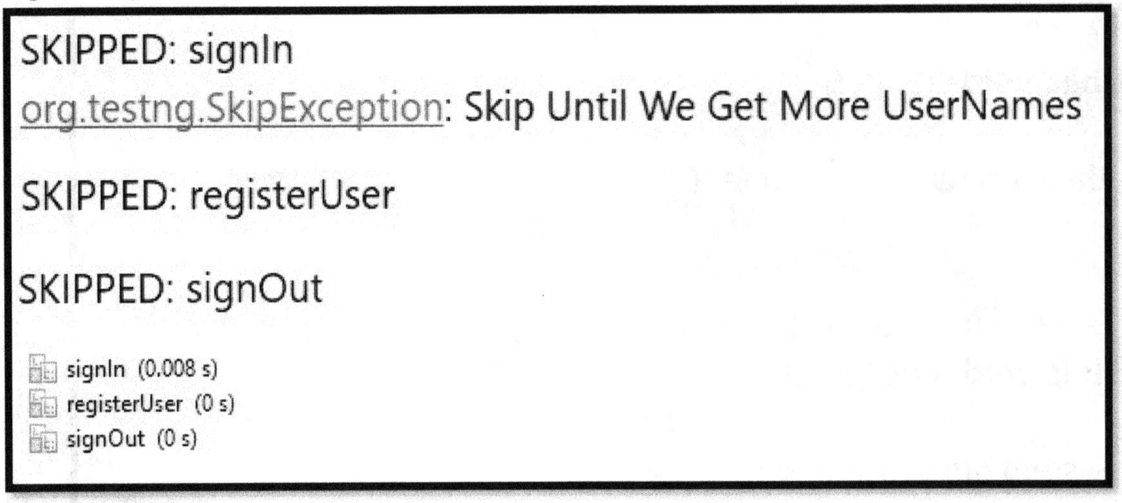

```
SKIPPED: signIn
org.testng.SkipException: Skip Until We Get More UserNames

SKIPPED: registerUser

SKIPPED: signOut

signIn (0.008 s)
registerUser (0 s)
signOut (0 s)
```

Figure 8.5 – Results From Executing A Skipped Method With A Dependency Attribute

Figure 8.4 shows the signIn() method is skipped using a SkipException via Line 37. However, the registerUser() and signOut() methods depend on the skipped method. Lines 40 and 46 reveal the syntax for dependsOnMethods Attribute for Test Annotation.

The Console shows all 3 methods are SKIPPED while TestNG Results tab shows a yellow icon for each method via Figure 8.5. Hypothetically, a user cannot be registered "2nd method / registerUser" if the application is not signed in "1st method / signIn". Furthermore, a user cannot sign out of the application "3rd method / signOut" if the application is not signed in "1st method".

Figure 8.2 is a good approach for Unit Testing while Figure 8.4 is an ideal approach for Dependency and/or Integration Testing. The following screenshot shows how to list multiple methods separated by a comma via dependsOnMethods().

Skype: rex.jones34
Twitter: @RexJonesII
Email: Rex.Jones@Test4Success.org
LinkedIn: https://www.linkedin.com/in/rexjones34

```
@Test ()
public void signIn ()
{
   System.out.println("Sign Into The Application");
}

@Test (dependsOnMethods = {"signIn"})
public void registerUser ()
{
   System.out.println("Register A User");
}

@Test (dependsOnMethods = {"signIn", "registerUser"})
public void signOut ()
{
   System.out.println("Sign Out Of The Application");
}
```

Figure 8.6 – Example Code With Multiple Methods via dependsOnMethods

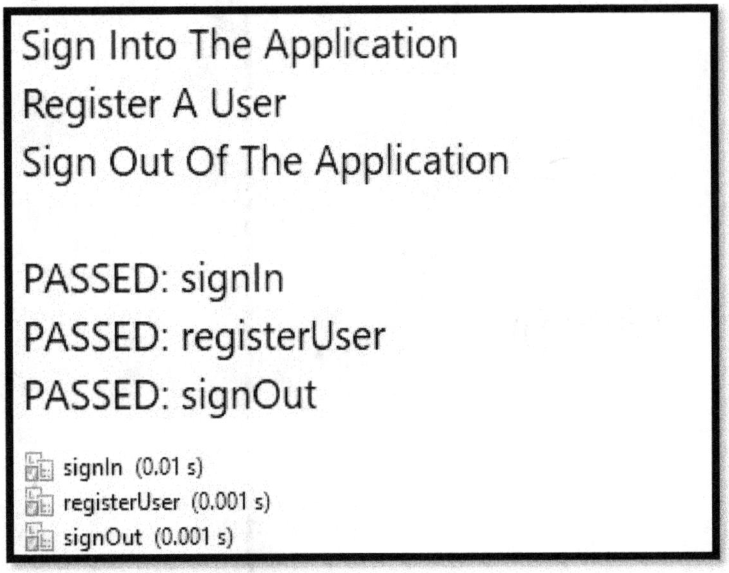

```
Sign Into The Application
Register A User
Sign Out Of The Application

PASSED: signIn
PASSED: registerUser
PASSED: signOut

signIn (0.01 s)
registerUser (0.001 s)
signOut (0.001 s)
```

Figure 8.7 – Results From Executing Multiple Methods via dependsOnMethods

Figure 8.6 shows multiple methods "signIn() and registerUser()" separated by a comma on Line 46. Notice, the signIn() method does not have a SkipException on Line 37. As a result, Figure 8.7 shows the Console with a print statement for each method and PASSED for all 3 methods "signIn, registerUser, signOut". In addition, the TestNG Results contain a green icon for each method.

Skype: rex.jones34
Twitter: @RexJonesII
Email: Rex.Jones@Test4Success.org
LinkedIn: https://www.linkedin.com/in/rexjones34

# Chapter 9
# Data Driven Testing

Data Driven Testing is when Test Data is stored in a data source then used as input for a Test Script. An automation engineer can have one Test Script that executes a combination of positive and/or negative test data. Sometimes Data Driven Testing is confused with Data Driven Framework. They are similar but the difference relies in receiving a Test Result after executing a Test Script. Data Driven Frameworks provide Test Data and receive a Test Result while Data Driven Testing only provide Test Data.

The most popular data source for providing Test Data is a spreadsheet such as Excel. However, TestNG can also utilize Java's Two-Dimensional Array as a data source. The following explain 2 layers for providing Test Data via Java's Two-Dimensional Array then show a couple of screenshots:

1. Add Test Data within a Two-Dimensional Array then return the Test Data via Java's method annotated by @DataProvider
2. Map @DataProvider Annotation to dataProvider Attribute within @Test Annotation

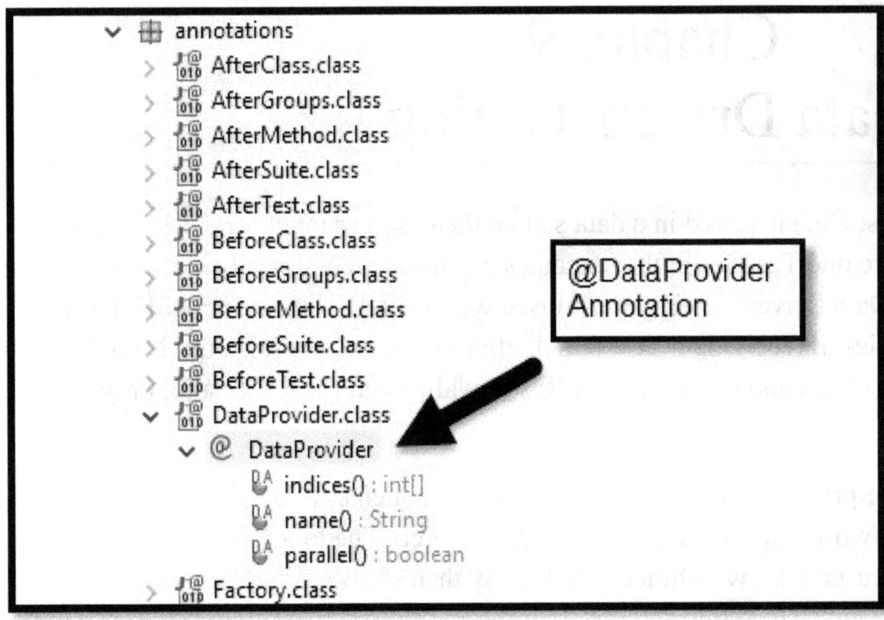


Figure 9.1 – DataProvider Annotation

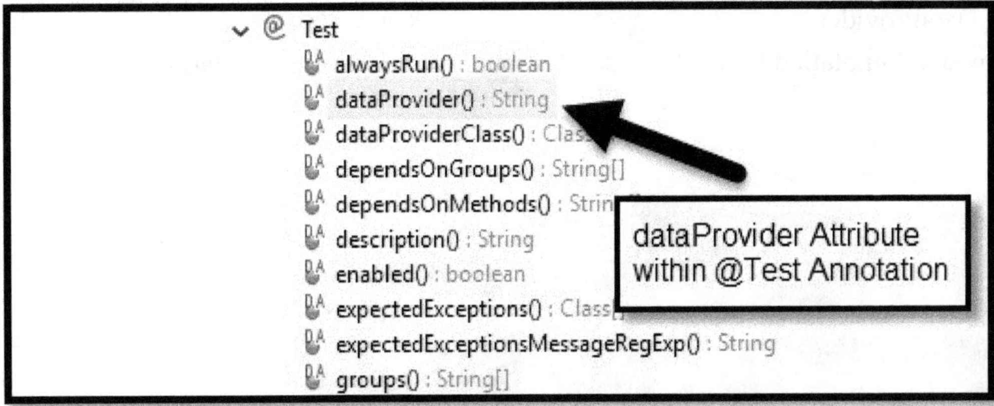


Figure 9.2 – dataProvider Attribute via Test Annotation

```
@DataProvider (name = "Credentials")
public Object [] [] provideData ()
{
   Object [] [] credentials = new Object [3] [2];

   credentials [0] [0] = "John_Doe@Tester.com";      credentials [0] [1] = "JohnDoe";
   credentials [1] [0] = "Jane_Doe@Tester.com";      credentials [1] [1] = "JaneDoe";
   credentials [2] [0] = "James_Doe@Tester.com";     credentials [2] [1] = "JamesDoe";

   return credentials;
}

@Test (dataProvider = "Credentials")
public void logIn (String email, String password)
{
   driver.findElement(By.linkText("Log in")).click();
   driver.findElement(By.xpath("//*[@id='Email']")).sendKeys(email);
   driver.findElement(By.xpath("//*[@id='Password']")).sendKeys(password);
   driver.findElement(By.xpath("//*[@type='submit']")).click();

   System.out.println("Email = " + email + "\n" + "Password = " + password);
}
```

Figure 9.3 – Automation Code Using @DataProvider Annotation And dataProvider Attribute

As mentioned in Chapter 3 – What Are Annotations, @DataProvider Annotation marks a method as providing data for a test method. Figure 9.1 shows the @DataProvider Annotation has 3 Attributes: indices, name, and parallel. The name Attribute is used to map @DataProvider Annotation to the dataProvider Attribute. In Figure 9.2, dataProvider is an attribute within the @Test Annotation which receives data from @DataProvider Annotation.

An example of the @DataProvider Annotation and dataProvider Attribute is located in Figure 9.3. Line 32 shows the @DataProvider Annotation while Line 44 shows the dataProvider Attribute. Both lines contain "Credentials" which maps the statements together. The test method via dataProvider Attribute needs to use the @DataProvider's name "Credentials" to receive Test Data. From a Java's perspective, the Test Data is located in a Two-Dimensional Object Array via Lines 35 - 41.

- Line 32 annotates the method with a @DataProvider Annotation named Credentials
- Line 33 declares the method with an Object [] [] Data Type named provideData
- Line 35 initializes the Two-Dimensional Array "credentials" with 3 rows and 2 columns
- Lines 37 – 39 contains the Test Data (email and password)
- Line 41 returns the credentials Test Data (email and password)
- Line 44 is a test method with a dataProvider Attribute equal to Credentials
- Line 45 declares a method named logIn with 2 String parameters (email and password)
- Line 48 enters email Test Data starting with Line 37 followed by Line 38 and Line 39
- Line 49 enters password Test Data starting with Line 37 followed by Line 38 and Line 39
- Line 52 prints the email and password Test Data

Additional information regarding Two-Dimensional Arrays and parameters are located in (Part 2) Java 4 Selenium WebDriver. The test method "logIn" runs each set of Test Data that provideData() method returns via credentials. String Parameters (email and password) via Line 45 receives the Test Data values while Lines 48 and 49 utilize the values. The following screenshot Figure 9.4 combined with Figure 9.3 is the complete automation code if you would like to execute Data Driven Testing:

```
13 public class WebShop
14 {
15     WebDriver driver;
16
17     @BeforeMethod
18     public void setUp () throws Exception
19     {
20         driver = new ChromeDriver ();
21         driver.manage().window().maximize();
22         driver.manage().timeouts().implicitlyWait(5, TimeUnit.SECONDS);
23         driver.get("http://demowebshop.tricentis.com/");
24     }
25
26     @AfterMethod
27     public void tearDown () throws Exception
28     {
29         driver.quit();
30     }
```

Figure 9.4 – Automation Code Using @BeforeMethod And @AfterMethod

System.setProperty() is not used in the previous and upcoming Selenium WebDriver automation code examples. It was bypassed after adding the drivers to Environment Variables. An exception shows up if the automation code is executed and drivers are not added to Environment Variables or System.setProperty() is not added before Line 20 "driver = **new** ChromeDriver ();". Here's an example that illustrates how to write System.setProperty for chromedriver.exe:

```
System.setProperty("webdriver.chrome.driver", "C:/Downloads/Drivers/chromedriver.exe");
```

Note: A document labeled "How To ByPass System.setProperty" can be downloaded at https://tinyurl.com/ByPass-System-setProperty that shows how to bypass System.setProperty().

In the previous screenshots, annotations @BeforeTest / @AfterTest were used for the examples. However, in Figure 9.4, @BeforeMethod / @AfterMethod is used to illustrate Data Driven Testing. According to their annotation execution order, an exception shows up for annotations @BeforeTest / @AfterTest. Recall the following definitions for @BeforeTest / @AfterTest and @BeforeMethod / @AfterMethod via Chapter 3 – Wat Are Annotations:

- @BeforeTest – The annotated method will run before any test method …
- @AfterTest – The annotated method will run after all the test methods…
- @BeforeMethod – The annotated method will run before each test method.
- @AfterMethod – The annotated method will run after each test method.

Here's the execution order for @BeforeTest / @AfterTest and @BeforeMethod / @AfterMethod:

- @BeforeTest / @AfterTest – browser opens, executes the first Test Data set, then the browser closes after executing the first Test Data set
  - credentials [0] [0] = "John_Doe@Tester.com";
  - credentials [0] [1] = "JohnDoe";
- @BeforeMethod / @AfterMethod – browser opens, executes the first Test Data set, then the browser closes after executing the first Test Data set. The browser opens again, executes the second Test Data set, then the browser closes after executing the second Test Data set. Execution repeats for third Test Data set (open browser, execute Test Data, close browser).

An exception shows up for @BeforeTest / @AfterTest because the browser does not re-open to execute the second and third Test Data set. However, the browser re-opens for @BeforeMethod / @AfterMethod. The following are results after executing Figures 9.3 and 9.4.

```
Email = John_Doe@Tester.com
Password = JohnDoe

Email = Jane_Doe@Tester.com
Password = JaneDoe

Email = James_Doe@Tester.com
Password = JamesDoe


PASSED: logIn("John_Doe@Tester.com", "JohnDoe")
PASSED: logIn("Jane_Doe@Tester.com", "JaneDoe")
PASSED: logIn("James_Doe@Tester.com", "JamesDoe")
```

Figure 9.5 – Console (Print Statements & Execution PASSED Results)

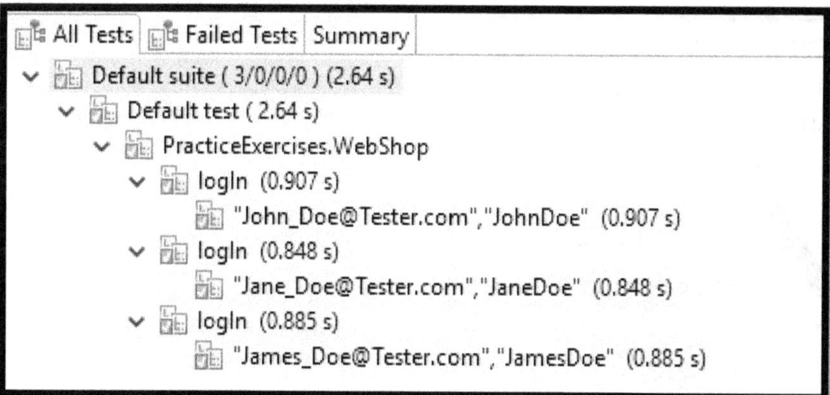


Figure 9.6 – TestNG Results

# Chapter 10
# Cross Browser Testing

Cross Browser Testing is a process of executing a Test Script on multiple browsers at the same time. In an ideal situation, all browsers provide the same experience to a user. Nevertheless, there are times when a browser responds differently and presents a defect. Cross Browser Testing verifies if the web applications are consistent on each browser.

An automation engineer can perform Cross Browser Testing using @DataProvider Annotation and dataProvider Attribute by adding the browsers via Two-Dimensional Array. However, a @Parameters Annotation and Parameterization through an xml file is another way to execute a Test Script across multiple browsers. In fact, the xml file has an ability to execute multiple Test Scripts on multiple browsers at the same time. By default, the xml file is named testng.xml. The following are screenshots for importing and automation code that uses @Parameters Annotation to process Cross Browser Testing:

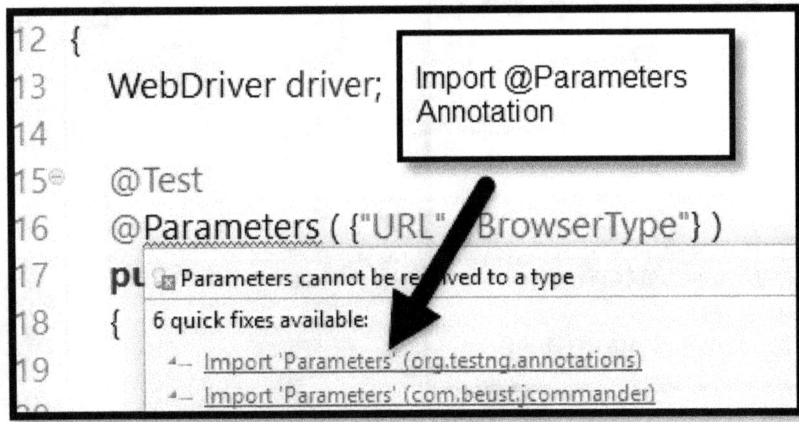


Figure 10.1 – Import @Parameters Annotation

Skype: rex.jones34
Twitter: @RexJonesII
Email: Rex.Jones@Test4Success.org
LinkedIn: https://www.linkedin.com/in/rexjones34

```
public class Books
{
  WebDriver driver;

  @Test
  @Parameters ( {"URL", "BrowserType"} )
  public void searchForBooks (String url, String browserType)
  {
    if (browserType.equalsIgnoreCase("chrome"))
    {
      driver = new ChromeDriver ();
    }
    else if (browserType.equalsIgnoreCase("firefox"))
    {
      driver = new FirefoxDriver ();
    }
    else
    {
      System.out.println("Chrome And Firefox Are The ONLY Available Browsers");
    }

    driver.get(url);
    driver.manage().timeouts().implicitlyWait(5, TimeUnit.SECONDS);
    driver.manage().window().maximize();

    System.out.println("\n" + "Open " + browserType);
    System.out.println("Search For Java, Selenium, And TestNG Books");
    System.out.println("Close " + browserType);
  }
```

Figure 10.2 – Automation Code Using @Parameters

There are multiple packages for @Parameters Annotation but Figure 10.1 shows package "org.testng.annotations" supports Cross Browser Testing. The @Parameters Annotation declares which parameter or parameters are passed to the test method. Here's a breakdown of Figure 10.2 which includes the parameters for @Parameters Annotation:

- Line 11 – displays a public class called Books
- Line 15 – displays @Test Annotation and sets the method as a test method. It doesn't matter which annotation is written first or second (Line 15 can be written after Line 16)
- Line 16 – displays @Parameters Annotation, URL parameter, and BrowserType parameter. Each parameter receives a value from the testng.xml and passes the value to Java's method searchForBooks on Line 17.
- Line 17 – Java method that receive the parameter values via String url and String browserType from Line 16.
- Lines 19 – 30 – Java's if-then-else statement that determines if the browser is Chrome, Firefox, or another browser type
    - Lines 19 – 22: driver uses ChromeDriver to control testing performed on Google Chrome if the parameter passes chrome
    - Line 23 – 26: driver uses FirefoxDriver to control testing performed on Firefox if the parameter passes firefox
    - Lines 27 – 30: prints a statement if the parameter does not pass chrome or firefox
- Line 32 – loads a new web page that is received from url parameter
- Line 36 – opens a browser that is received from browserType parameter
- Line 38 – closes the browser that is received from browserType parameter

Up to this point, examples, executions, etc. have been carried out from a class file. In this example, the values within Books class are received from testng.xml file. According to Next Generation Java ™ Testing TestNG and Advanced Concepts, an XML file captures a given configuration of classes, test, methods, parameters, exclusions, and so on (page 435). The following are steps and screenshots for converting a class to an xml file:

Steps to convert a class to xml:

1. Right click a class “i.e., Books” within Project Explorer
2. Select TestNG
3. Select Convert to TestNG
4. Click Finish to generate an xml file

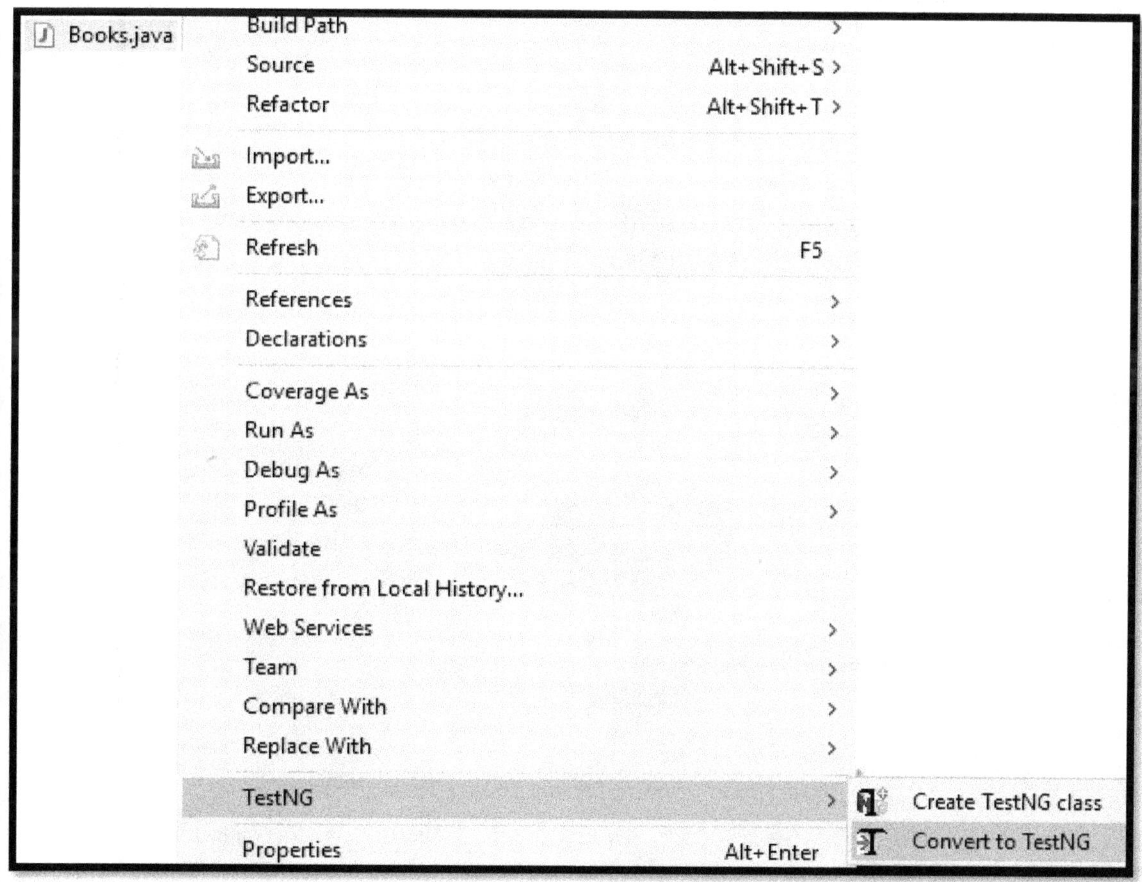


Figure 10.3 – Right Click A Class Then Convert To TestNG

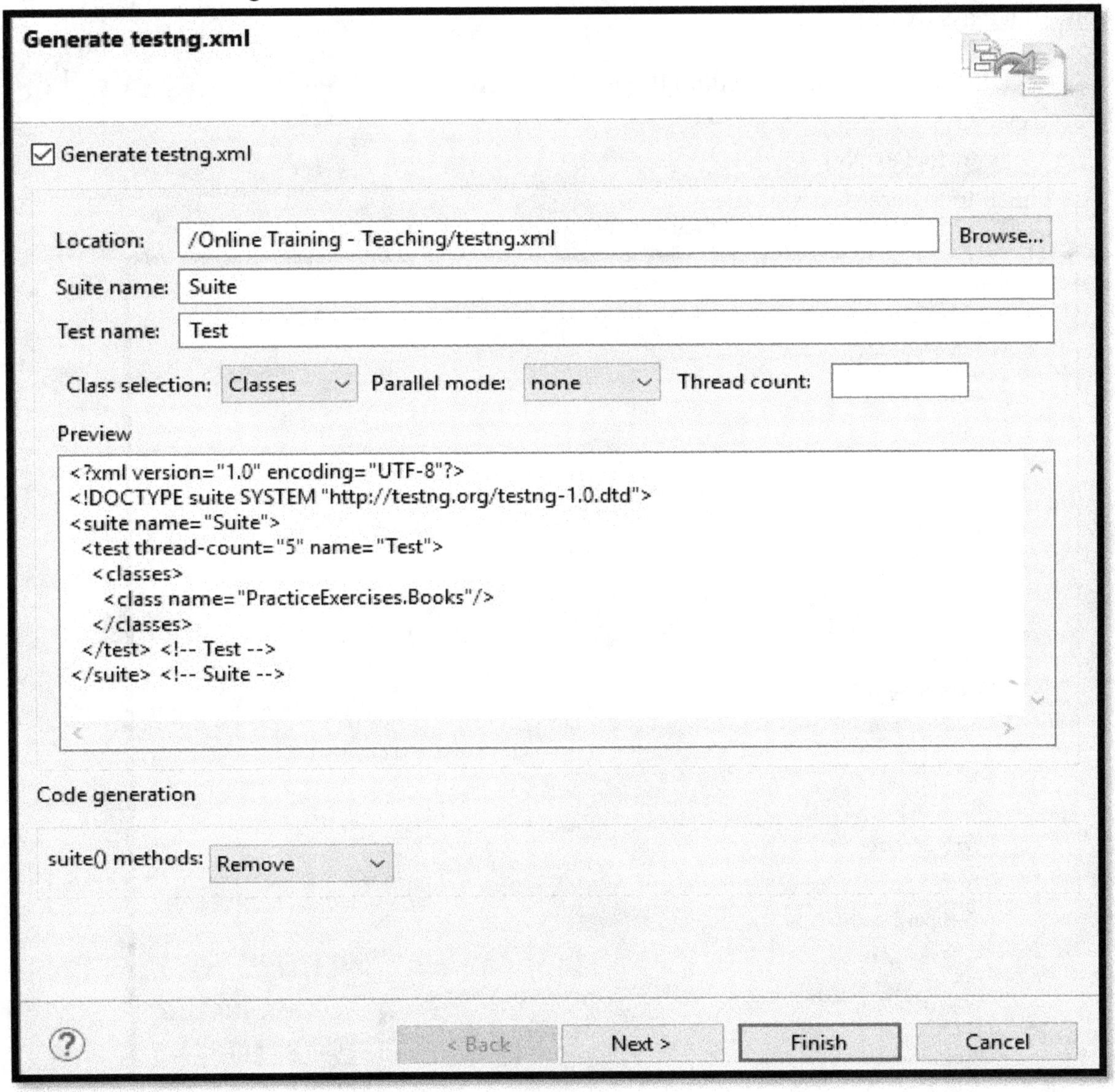

**Generate testng.xml**

☑ Generate testng.xml

Location: /Online Training - Teaching/testng.xml Browse...

Suite name: Suite

Test name: Test

Class selection: Classes Parallel mode: none Thread count:

Preview

```
<?xml version="1.0" encoding="UTF-8"?>
<!DOCTYPE suite SYSTEM "http://testng.org/testng-1.0.dtd">
<suite name="Suite">
  <test thread-count="5" name="Test">
    <classes>
      <class name="PracticeExercises.Books"/>
    </classes>
  </test> <!-- Test -->
</suite> <!-- Suite -->
```

Code generation

suite() methods: Remove

< Back Next > Finish Cancel

Figure 10.4 – Generate An xml File

Skype: rex.jones34
Twitter: @RexJonesII
Email: Rex.Jones@Test4Success.org
LinkedIn: https://www.linkedin.com/in/rexjones34

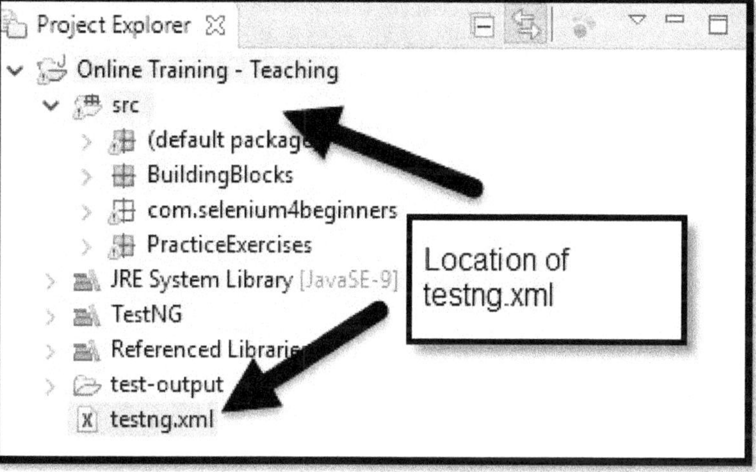


Figure 10.5 – Location of testng.xml

```
<?xml version="1.0" encoding="UTF-8"?>
<!DOCTYPE suite SYSTEM "http://testng.org/testng-1.0.dtd">
<suite name="Suite">
  <test thread-count="5" name="Test">
    <classes>
      <class name="PracticeExercises.Books"/>
    </classes>
  </test> <!-- Test -->
</suite> <!-- Suite -->
```

Figure 10.6 – Default xml File After Converting Books Class

The xml file Location, xml file name, Suite name, and Test name can be changed before clicking the Finish button. Figure 10.5 shows the testng.xml location after clicking the Finish button. Updates can be made in Project Explorer to modify the xml file location and name. The Suite and Test name can be modified within the xml file. Here's a breakdown of the testng.xml file to explain XML Tags via Figure 10.6:

- Line 2 – DOCTYPE validates the XML file by ensuring the syntax is appropriate.
- Line 3 – a <suite> tag which is the root tag with name as the only required attribute. The <suite> tag contains at least one <test> tag.
- Line 4 – a <test> tag that has name as the only required attribute. Attribute thread-count indicates a number of threads if running parallel mode. The <test> tag contains at least one <class> within <classes> tag.
- Line 5 – a <classes> tag allows Java classes to be defined for execution.
- Line 6 – a <class> tag that has name as the only required attribute. The syntax is package name dot class name within double quotes. Additional classes can be included for execution between <classes> tag
- Line 7 – closing </classes> tag for the opening <classes> tag on Line 5
- Line 8 - closing </test> tag for the opening <test> tag on Line 4. A comment labeled <!— Test --> is added at the end of the closing </test> tag.
- Line 9 - closing </suite> tag for the opening <suite> tag on Line 3. A comment labeled <!— Suite --> is added at the end of the closing </suite> tag.

The following screenshot via Figure 10.7 combined with Figure 10.2 is the actual code to process Cross Browser Testing. Add System.setProperty() for each driver before Lines 21 and 25 via Figure 10.2 if the drivers have not been added to Environment Variables.

```
<!DOCTYPE suite SYSTEM "http://testng.org/testng-1.0.dtd">

<suite name="Cross Browser Testing On Multiple Browsers">

  <parameter name = "URL" value = "http://tinyurl.com/Rex-Allen-Jones-Books"/>

 <test name="Test On Chrome">
  <parameter name = "BrowserType" value = "Chrome"> </parameter>
  <classes>
    <class name="PracticeExercises.Books"/>
  </classes>
 </test> <!-- Test -->

 <test name="Test On Firefox">
  <parameter name = "BrowserType" value = "Firefox"/>
  <classes>
    <class name="PracticeExercises.Books"/>
  </classes>
 </test> <!-- Test -->

</suite> <!-- Suite -->
```

Figure 10.7 – Customized xml File To Process Cross Browser Testing For Books

The updated XML file removes some information but includes a required <parameter> tag to process Cross Browser Testing. Optional updates were made to rename the Suite and Test. The following explains each update via Figure 10.7:

- Line 4 – suite name changed to Cross Browser Testing On Multiple Browsers
- Line 6 – a <parameter> tag that has name and value as required attributes. Both attributes are passed to the @Parameters Annotation in Books class. A value of http://tinyurl.com/Rex-Allen-Jones-Books is passed to the URL parameter
- Line 8 – test name changed to Test On Chrome
- Line 9 – a <parameter> tag that has BrowserType as the name and Chrome as the value. Both attributes are passed to the @Parameters Annotation
- Line 15 – test name changed to Test On Firefox
- Line 9 – a <parameter> tag that has BrowserType as the name and Firefox as the value. Both attributes are passed to the @Parameters Annotation

Notice, there are 2 <test> tags but 3 <parameter> tags. Line 6 <parameter> tag placed is within the <suite> tag because both <test> tags use the same URL value. However, the <parameter> on Lines 9 and 16 contain different values for loading a specific browser. The following screenshots show how to execute an xml file and results after execute testng.xml:

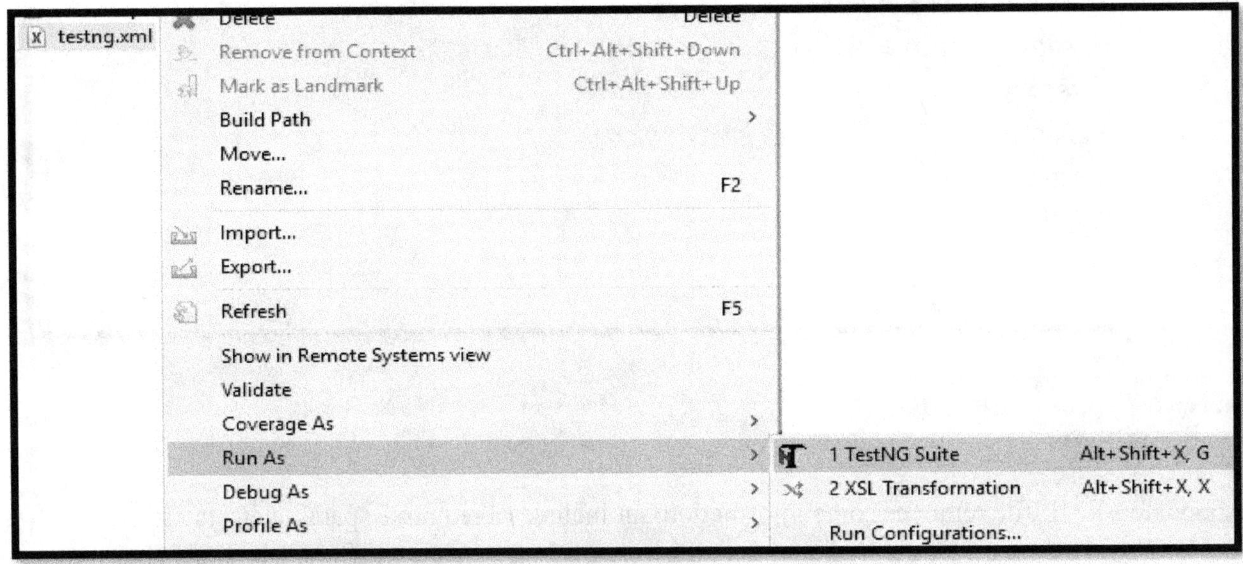


Figure 10.8 – Right Click testing.xml Then Execute / Run

```
Open Chrome
Search For Java, Selenium, And TestNG Books
Close Chrome

Open Firefox
Search For Java, Selenium, And TestNG Books
Close Firefox


===============================================
Cross Browser Testing On Multiple Browsers
Total tests run: 2, Failures: 0, Skips: 0
===============================================
```

Figure 10.9 – Cross Browser Testing Console Results

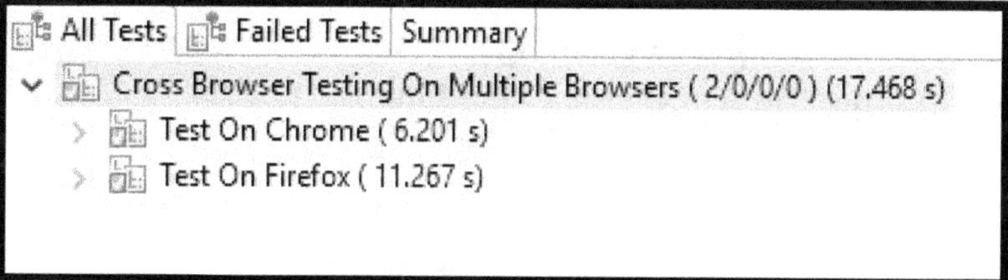


Figure 10.10 – Minimize Cross Browser Testing TestNG Results

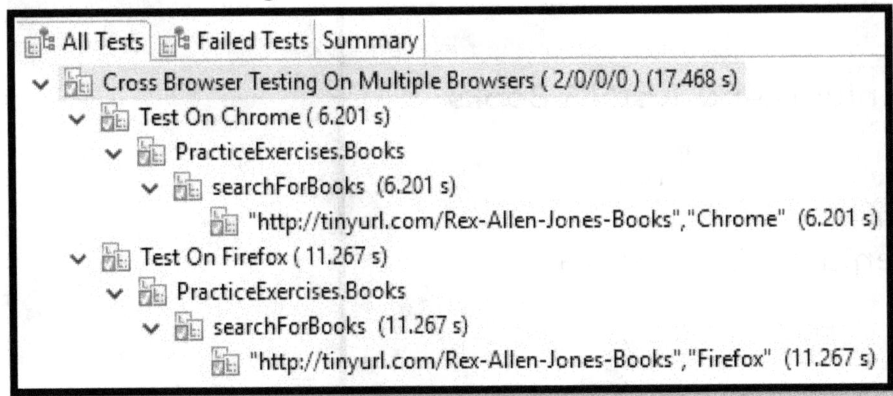


Figure 10.11 – Maximize Cross Browser Testing TestNG Results

Figure 10.9 shows the Console Results. The screenshot illustrates execution was processed on Chrome and Firefox. Print statements show each browser was opened, books were searched, then the browser was closed followed by the Suite Name and 2 runs. Figure 10.10 and Figure 10.11 show the TestNG Results.

For Figure 10.10, the top row is the Suite Name "Cross Browser Testing On Multiple Browsers". Afterwards the Test Name is displayed for Chrome "Test On Chrome" and Firefox "Test On Firefox". For Figure 10.11, the last row for Chrome and Firefox shows both values: URL and BrowserType. The URL and BrowserType values were passed from testng.xml to the Java class to process Cross Browser Testing.

# Conclusion

TestNG is a Java test framework influenced by JUnit. JUnit is the most popular framework but TestNG is the most powerful framework. Both frameworks contain assertions and annotations that are required for testing an application. However, TestNG added more features that facilitate all sorts of testing. Some of the test types are Unit Testing, Dependency Testing, Data Driven Testing, and Cross Browser Testing. According to Next Generation Java ™ Testing TestNG and Advanced Concepts, some additional features of TestNG include the following:

- Automatically identify and run JUnit test
- Generate reports in HTML and XML
- Trace code that handles exceptions
- Group test methods and specify groups that contain other groups

# Resources


1. TestNG
   http://testng.org/doc/documentation-main.html#annotations

2. Tutorials Point
   https://www.tutorialspoint.com/software_testing_dictionary/dependency_testing.htm

3. Next Generation Java ™ Testing
   TestNG and Advanced Concepts
   Cédric Beust | Hani Suleiman


Skype: rex.jones34
Twitter: @RexJonesII
Email: Rex.Jones@Test4Success.org
LinkedIn: https://www.linkedin.com/in/rexjones34

# Download PDF Version

The PDF Version of this book is available to you at the following link:

https://tinyurl.com/Getting-Started-With-TestNG

If this book was helpful, can you leave a favorable review?

https://tinyurl.com/TestNG-Getting-Started

Thanks in advance,

Rex Allen Jones II

Rex Allen Jones II

# Books by Rex Jones II

www.tinyurl.com/Rex-Allen-Jones-books

1. **Free Book** Absolute Beginner
   (Part 1) You Must Learn VBScript for QTP/UFT
   Don't Ignore The Language For Functional Automation Testing

2. (Part 2) You Must Learn VBScript for QTP/UFT
   Don't Ignore The Language For Functional Automation Testing

3. **Free Book** Absolute Beginner
   (Part 1) Java 4 Selenium WebDriver
   Come Learn How To Program For Automation Testing

4. (Part 2) Java 4 Selenium WebDriver
   Come Learn How To Program For Automation Testing

5. **Free Book** Absolute Beginner
   (Part 1) Selenium WebDriver for Functional Automation Testing
   Your Beginners Guide

6. Getting Started With TestNG
   A Java Test Framework

Skype: rex.jones34
Twitter: @RexJonesII
Email: Rex.Jones@Test4Success.org
LinkedIn: https://www.linkedin.com/in/rexjones34

# Books by Rex Jones II

3 Tips To Master Selenium Within 30 Days
http://tinyurl.com/3-Tips-For-Selenium

Free Webinars, Videos, and Live Trainings
http://tinyurl.com/Free-QTP-UFT-Selenium

# Sign Up To Receive

1. 3 Tips To Master Selenium Within 30 Days
   http://tinyurl.com/3-Tips-For-Selenium

2. 3 Tips To Master QTP/UFT Within 30 Days
   http://tinyurl.com/3-Tips-For-QTP-UFT

3. Free Webinars, Videos, and Live Trainings
   http://tinyurl.com/Free-QTP-UFT-Selenium

Skype: rex.jones34
Twitter: @RexJonesII
Email: Rex.Jones@Test4Success.org
LinkedIn: https://www.linkedin.com/in/rexjones34

www.ingramcontent.com/pod-product-compliance
Lightning Source LLC
Chambersburg PA
CBHW060206060326
40690CB00018B/4274

* 9 7 8 1 7 2 6 3 9 4 4 7 5 *